From a GRANDFATHER'S HEART

MEMORIES for my GRANDCHILD

RUBY OAKS

CASTLE POINT BOOKS
NEW YORK

The Castle Point Books trademark is owned by Castle Point Publications, LLC.
Castle Point books are published and distributed by St. Martin's Press.

Cover and interior design by Tara Long
Images used under license from Shutterstock.com

ISBN 978-1-250-22743-0 (hardcover)

Our books may be purchased in bulk for promotional, educational, or business use.
Please contact your local bookseller or the Macmillan Corporate and Premium Sales Department
at 1-800-221-7945, extension 5442, or by email at MacmillanSpecialMarkets@macmillan.com.

First Edition: May 2019

10 9 8 7 6 5 4 3 2 1

Contents

INTRODUCTION

Maybe you have some favorite stories that you love to tell time and time again. And maybe there are a few tales that you have kept close to your heart through the years. All of your stories make up the book of your life. They have made you who you are today, and it's time to share your life's worth of lessons with a very special grandchild.

Using the prompts in this book makes it easy to capture some of the most important moments. You may even remember a few fond and favorite times that were tucked away and forgotten! Simply fill in the blanks, one line at a time, to walk down memory lane—and give your grandchild a new window into the real you (and some heritage he or she may not yet know).

You can work on this book on your own, perhaps over your morning cup of coffee, or complete it with loved ones at family gatherings. Or try a bit of both. When the pages are filled, you will have a new keepsake to share with your grandchild. And as you read it together, you will create another beautiful memory that will bring you even closer to each other.

WHERE IT
ALL STARTED

THE STORY OF MY BIRTH

BELIEVE IT OR NOT, THE YEAR WAS: _ _ _ _ _ _ _ _ _ _ _ _ _ !

MONTH & DAY: TIME:

_   _ _ _ _ _ _ _ _ _ _ _ _ _ _ _

WHERE I WAS BORN:

_ _

A PHOTO OF ME AS A BABY:

THE STORY BEHIND MY NAME

My full name:

[   ]

HOW OR WHY MY NAME WAS CHOSEN:

- -

HOW I FELT ABOUT MY NAME AS A CHILD:

- -

- -

NICKNAMES I'VE HAD
OVER THE YEARS:

- - - - - - - - - - - - - - - - - - -

- - - - - - - - - - - - - - - - - - -

- - - - - - - - - - - - - - - - - - -

- - - - - - - - - - - - - - - - - - -

THE
STORY
OF *You & Me*

THE NAME I *THOUGHT*
YOU WOULD CALL ME:

THE NAME YOU
DECIDED TO CALL ME:

IN THE HEADLINES THAT YEAR

HISTORIC EVENTS:

- -

- -

- -

The #1 song:

SOME FADS:

- -

- -

POPULAR ENTERTAINERS AND CELEBRITIES:

- -

- -

- -

Together Time

DON'T KNOW THE ANSWERS?
HAVE YOUR GRANDCHILD SEARCH WITH YOU ONLINE.

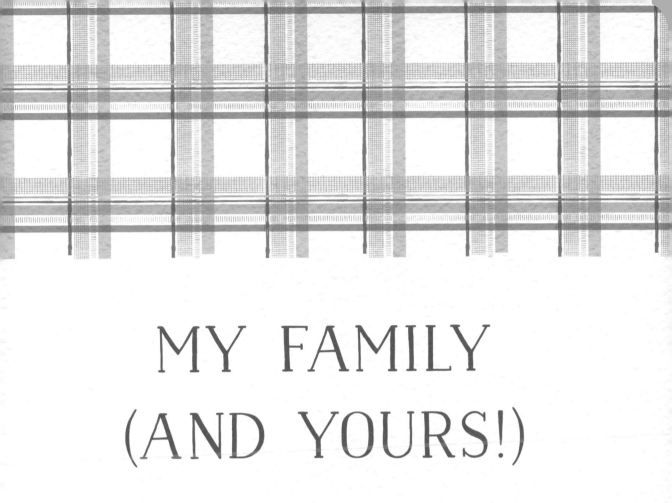

MY FAMILY
(AND YOURS!)

MY ANCESTORS

COUNTRIES MY ANCESTORS CAME FROM:

....

....

WHAT I KNOW ABOUT MY FAMILY NAME:

....

....

....

AN INTERESTING FAMILY LEGEND:

....

....

....

....

CELEBRATIONS OF OUR HERITAGE

FAMILY FOODS:

FAMILY TRADITIONS:

A family saying:

"

"

My Family Tree

Together Time

ADD THE FIRST
PHOTOGRAPH TO THE TREE,
THEN SEE HOW MANY MORE
PICTURES OF THAT RELATIVE YOU
AND YOUR GRANDCHILD CAN
FIND IN OTHER FAMILY ALBUMS.

MEMORIES OF MY MOTHER

MY MOTHER'S NAME:

- -

[*What I called her:*]

THINGS SHE WAS GOOD AT OR LIKED TO DO:

- -

- -

- -

ONE THING SHE TAUGHT ME:

- -

- -

- -

- -

A FOND OR FUNNY MEMORY:

MY MOTHER & ME:

MEMORIES OF MY FATHER

MY FATHER'S NAME:

- -

[*What I called him:*]

THINGS HE WAS GOOD AT OR LIKED TO DO:

- -

- -

- -

ONE THING HE TAUGHT ME:

- -

- -

- -

A FOND OR FUNNY MEMORY:

- -

- -

- -

- -

- -

- -

- -

MY FATHER & ME:

MY SIBLING(S)

WHAT I'D LIKE YOU TO KNOW ABOUT MY SIBLING(S):

A PHOTO OF MY SIBLING(S):

THE NAMES OF MY SISTERS AND BROTHERS
AND A LITTLE INFO ABOUT EACH:

[   ]

- -

- -

[   ]

- -

- -

[   ]

- -

- -

[   ]

- -

- -

MEET MY COUSINS

ON MY MOTHER'S SIDE:

- -

ON MY FATHER'S SIDE:

- -

OUR FAVORITE WAY TO SPEND TIME TOGETHER:

- -

MY COUSINS & ME:

MORE CLOSE RELATIVES

NAME/RELATIONSHIP

- - - - - - - - - - - - - - - - - - / - - - - - - - - - - - - - - - - -

A FAVORITE MEMORY:

- -

- -

NAME/RELATIONSHIP

- - - - - - - - - - - - - - - - - - / - - - - - - - - - - - - - - - - -

A FAVORITE MEMORY:

- -

- -

NAME/RELATIONSHIP

- - - - - - - - - - - - - - - - - - / - - - - - - - - - - - - - - - - -

A FAVORITE MEMORY:

- -

- -

MY GRANDPARENTS & ME

My Mother's Parents

THEIR NAMES:

------------------------------ / ------------------------------

[*What I called them:*]

WHAT WE DID TOGETHER:

WHAT THEY TAUGHT ME ABOUT BEING A GRANDPARENT:

My Father's Parents

THEIR NAMES:

_____ / _____

What I called them:

[ ]

WHAT WE DID TOGETHER:

_____

_____

WHAT THEY TAUGHT ME ABOUT BEING A GRANDPARENT:

_____

_____

_____

_____

FAMILY STORIES & SECRETS

AN UNUSUAL STORY ABOUT OUR FAMILY:

- -

- -

- -

Shhhh...   A FAMILY SECRET YOU MAY NOT KNOW:

- -

- -

A SECRET ABOUT **MY** LIFE (DON'T TELL YOUR PARENTS!):

- -

- -

- -

Together Time

GO ONLINE WITH YOUR GRANDCHILD
TO TRACE YOUR ROOTS. YOU MAY FIND SOME FAMOUS
(OR INFAMOUS) PEOPLE IN YOUR FAMILY TREE!

WHEN I
WAS A KID

WHAT I WAS LIKE

I LOOKED LIKE THIS:

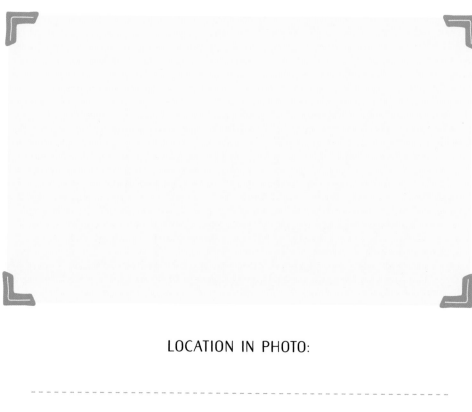

LOCATION IN PHOTO:

- -

AGE/YEAR:

- / -

My position in my family:

YOUNGEST   MIDDLE   OLDEST   I WAS AN ONLY CHILD

MY BEST TRAITS:

MY WORST TRAITS:

MY ROLES IN THE FAMILY (HARD WORKER, ARTIST, JOKESTER, ETC.):

FAVORITE THINGS AS A CHILD

FAVORITE TOYS AND GAMES:

FAVORITE SHOWS OR MOVIES:

Favorite books:

FAVORITE SONGS:

FAVORITE ACTIVITIES AND HOBBIES:

FAVORITE SPORTS AND TEAMS:

FAVORITE CELEBRITIES AND HEROES:

- -

FAVORITE RELATIVE: { *Favorite gift:*

-            }

FAVORITE FOODS/BEVERAGES:

- -

FAVORITE THING TO COLLECT:

- -

FAVORITE SLANG OR SAYINGS:

" -

- "

Together Time

ASK YOUR GRANDCHILD WHAT HIS OR
HER FAVORITES ARE TODAY. WRITE THEM BESIDE
YOUR OWN AND COMPARE NOTES!

THE BEST OF FRIENDS

Very First Friends

NAMES:

WHAT WE DID TOGETHER:

ONE FAVORITE MEMORY:

Childhood Buddies

NAMES:

WHAT WE DID TOGETHER:

ONE FAVORITE MEMORY:

Middle School Pals

NAMES:

- -

WHAT WE DID TOGETHER:

- -

ONE FAVORITE MEMORY:

- -

High School Friends

NAMES:

- -

WHAT WE DID TOGETHER:

- -

ONE FAVORITE MEMORY:

- -

MY CHILDHOOD PETS

PET NAME:

- -

BEST & WORST TRAITS:

- -

- -

- -

- -

PET NAME:

- -

BEST & WORST TRAITS:

- -

- -

- -

{ *A pet I wanted but never got and why:*

- -

- }

HOME, SWEET HOME

WHEN I WAS GROWING UP,
THIS WAS ONE OF THE PLACES I LIVED:

MY ADDRESS:

- -

YEARS I LIVED THERE:

- -

WHERE I SPENT THE MOST TIME WHEN I LIVED THERE:

A FAVORITE MEMORY OF THIS HOME:

My Bedroom

I WOULD DESCRIBE MY CHILDHOOD BEDROOM THIS WAY:

MY LIFE AS A KID

MY BEDTIME:

- -

MY WAKE-UP TIME:

- -

OUR MEALS (WHEN, WHERE, AND WHAT WE ATE):

- -

- -

- -

- -

- -

MY FAVORITE THING TO WEAR:

THE STORY OF *You & Me*

ONE THING I **DID**
THAT YOU DON'T:

ONE THING I **DIDN'T**
DO THAT YOU DO:

MY CHORES:

I WAS ALWAYS DOING THIS:

MY BIGGEST CHALLENGES

MY FIRST BROKEN HEART:

THE FIRST LOVED ONE I LOST:

[*A special item that got lost or broken:*]

MY ADVICE FOR DEALING WITH
THE LOSSES THAT HAPPEN IN LIFE:

One challenge I faced in school:

- -

WHAT I DID ABOUT IT:

- -

- -

WHAT HAPPENED AS A RESULT:

- -

- -

One challenge I faced at home:

- -

WHAT I DID ABOUT IT:

- -

- -

WHAT HAPPENED AS A RESULT:

- -

IMPORTANT MOMENTS IN HISTORY

[*One historic event from my childhood:*]

WHAT I REMEMBER ABOUT IT:

- -

- -

HOW I FEEL ABOUT IT NOW:

- -

- -

OTHER HISTORIC MOMENTS I LIVED THROUGH AS A KID:

- -

- -

- -

STORIES
FROM SCHOOL

SCHOOL-DAY BASICS

SCHOOLS I ATTENDED:

NUMBER OF GRADUATES IN
MY HIGH SCHOOL CLASS:

WHAT I WORE TO SCHOOL:

HOW I GOT TO AND FROM SCHOOL:

WHAT I ATE FOR LUNCH:

FAVORITE TEACHERS

Best elementary school teacher:

[   ]

HERE'S WHY:

- -

- -

Best middle school teacher:

[   ]

HERE'S WHY:

- -

- -

Best high school teacher:

[   ]

HERE'S WHY:

- -

- -

BEST & WORST SUBJECTS

MY FAVORITE CLASSES IN SCHOOL:

HERE'S WHY:

MY LEAST FAVORITE CLASSES IN SCHOOL:

HERE'S WHY:

Together Time

TALK ABOUT HOW
SCHOOL SUBJECTS HAVE
CHANGED OVER THE YEARS.

HOW I WOULD
DESCRIBE MY GRADES:

GOOD

AVERAGE

POOR

LET'S NOT DISCUSS IT!

AFTER-SCHOOL ACTIVITIES

HOW I FELT ABOUT HOMEWORK AND TESTS:

{ *In the evenings, this is how I passed the time:*

}

I WAS A MEMBER OF THESE CLUBS OR GROUPS:

SCHOOL-DAY MEMORIES

A HAPPY MEMORY:

A funny memory:

A TIME THAT I GOT IN TROUBLE:

PICTURE DAYS

My best school picture:

My worst school picture:

WHAT I WAS LIKE AS A TEENAGER

Weekend plans:

{
_____

_____

_____
}

MY GREATEST WORRY OR FEAR:

_____

_____

_____

_____

WHAT BROUGHT ME JOY:

_____

_____

_____

_____

MY FIRST JOB

MY AGE AT THE TIME I STARTED:

- -

THE REASON I STARTED WORKING:

- -

- -

MY RESPONSIBILITIES:

- -

- -

- -

How much I earned:

WHAT I LEARNED FROM THAT JOB:

- -

- -

- -

GROWING UP WITH GOALS

MY CHILDHOOD DREAM JOB:

OTHER JOBS I CONSIDERED OR TRIED:

[*My favorite job over the years:*]

MY EXPERIENCE WITH THE MILITARY:

MY MOST SHINING SCHOOL MOMENTS

THIS ACHIEVEMENT MADE MY FAMILY PROUD:

THIS ACHIEVEMENT MADE ME PROUD:

SOME OTHER AWARDS OR HONORS I RECEIVED:

Together Time

SHOW YOUR GRANDCHILD SOME PHOTOS
OF THESE MOMENTS. ALSO, SHARE WHAT
MAKES YOU PROUD OF HIM OR HER.

ADULTS WHO INSPIRED ME

MOTIVATING COACHES & LEADERS:

Meaningful Mentors & Instructors:

THE STORY OF You & Me

THIS IS SOMETHING
I ADMIRE ABOUT YOU:

BEING YOUR GRANDFATHER
HAS INSPIRED ME TO:

LIKE A SECOND SET OF PARENTS:

YOUR
GRANDMOTHER
& ME

HOW I MET YOUR GRANDMOTHER

DATE WE MET:

- -

WHERE WE MET:

- -

OUR AGES AT THE TIME:

- - - - - - - - - - - / - - - - - - - - - - -

MY FIRST IMPRESSION OF HER:

- -

Our first date:

- -

- -

- -

A FAVORITE PHOTO OF HER:

HER JOBS, HOBBIES, & INTERESTS:

YOUR GRANDMOTHER'S FAMILY

COUNTRIES HER ANCESTORS CAME FROM:

- -

- -

- -

AN INTERESTING FAMILY LEGEND:

- -

- -

- -

- -

- -

- -

Together Time

LOOK THROUGH SOME OLD PHOTOS
FROM THIS SIDE OF THE FAMILY. WHAT DO THESE
RELATIVES HAVE IN COMMON WITH YOUR GRANDCHILD,
IN LOOKS AND PERSONALITY?

Family foods & traditions:

THE STORY OF WHEN I MET HER FAMILY:

FALLING IN LOVE

I KNEW YOUR GRANDMOTHER WAS THE GIRL FOR ME WHEN:

OUR FAVORITE DATE SPOTS:

HOW I PROPOSED:

OUR WEDDING

DATE/PLACE

---------------------------- / ----------------------------

OUR AGES AT THE TIME:

---------------------------- / ----------------------------

A FAVORITE MEMORY OF OUR WEDDING DAY:

A FAVORITE WEDDING PHOTO:

OUR CHILDREN

THE NAMES AND BIRTHDAYS OF ALL MY CHILDREN:

-------------------------------   -------------------------------

-------------------------------   -------------------------------

-------------------------------   -------------------------------

-------------------------------   -------------------------------

-------------------------------   -------------------------------

-------------------------------   -------------------------------

HERE WE ARE TOGETHER:

WHAT WE LOVED TO DO MOST AS A FAMILY
WHEN YOUR MOM/DAD WAS GROWING UP:

- -

- -

- -

- -

- -

HOW WE SPEND TIME TOGETHER NOW:

- -

- -

- -

- -

- -

Together Time

TELL YOUR GRANDCHILD WHICH
AUNT OR UNCLE HE OR SHE MOST RESEMBLES
IN LOOKS, IN PERSONALITY, OR BOTH!

FUN FACTS ABOUT YOUR PARENT

Here's how I remember your mom/dad.

AS A BABY:

AS A CHILD:

AS A TEEN:

ONE THING YOU PROBABLY NEVER KNEW ABOUT YOUR MOM/DAD:

[*My age at the time your mom/dad was born:*]

WHEN YOUR PARENTS MET, MY FIRST IMPRESSION WAS:

YOU & YOUR GRANDMOTHER

SOME PERSONALITY TRAITS YOU SHARE:

SOME THINGS YOUR GRANDMOTHER LOVES ABOUT YOU:

A FAVORITE PHOTO OF YOU AND YOUR GRANDMOTHER:

CELEBRATIONS
& TRADITIONS

MY FAVORITE HOLIDAY

[*As a child, my favorite holiday was:*]

HERE'S WHY:

AS AN ADULT,
MY FAVORITE HOLIDAY IS:

THE STORY OF *You & Me*

MY FAVORITE HOLIDAY
TO SPEND WITH YOU IS:

HERE'S WHY:

HERE'S WHY:

BIRTHDAY TRADITIONS

HOW WE CELEBRATED WHEN I WAS A KID:

MY FONDEST CHILDHOOD PARTY:

SOME MEMORABLE PRESENTS
FROM MY CHILDHOOD:

THE STORY OF *You & Me*

A FAVORITE BIRTHDAY
PRESENT YOU GAVE ME:

HOW I LIKE TO CELEBRATE TODAY:

NEW YEAR'S EVE

HOW WE CELEBRATED WHEN I WAS A KID:

{ *My best New Year's Eve as an adult:* }

SOME RESOLUTIONS I MADE OVER THE YEARS:

SOME RESOLUTIONS I ACTUALLY KEPT:

FOURTH OF JULY

HOW WE CELEBRATED WHEN I WAS A KID:

- -

- -

MY FAVORITE INDEPENDENCE DAY TRADITION:

- -

- -

THE BEST FIREWORKS DISPLAY
I HAVE EVER SEEN:

- -

- -

PICNIC FOODS I LOVE:

- -

- -

HALLOWEEN

HOW WE CELEBRATED WHEN I WAS A KID:

SOME MEMORABLE CHILDHOOD COSTUMES:

[*My favorite Halloween candy is:*]

MY PREFERRED WAY TO CELEBRATE AS AN ADULT:

THANKSGIVING

HOW WE CELEBRATED WHEN I WAS A KID:

....

....

THE FOODS ON OUR HOLIDAY TABLE:

....

....

....

AFTER DINNER, WE WOULD:

....

....

....

MY FAVORITE THING ABOUT THANKSGIVING NOW:

....

....

....

WINTER WONDERS

My favorite wintertime holiday as a child:

HOW WE CELEBRATED IT:

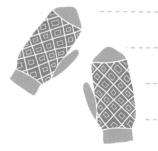

_____

_____

_____

_____

_____

THE WAYS I LIKE TO CELEBRATE WITH **YOU**:

_____

_____

_____

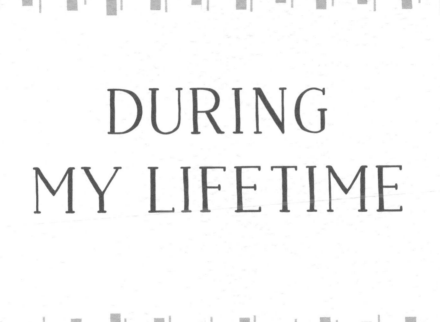

DURING MY LIFETIME

THE COST OF LIVING

A MOVIE TICKET:

A CANDY BAR:

A GALLON OF MILK:

A GALLON OF GAS:

MY FIRST VEHICLE:

MY FIRST HOUSE:

MY FIRST JOB'S WAGES:

TEEN TRENDS & FADS

WHAT I WORE:

THE KIND OF CAR I WANTED:

THE KIND OF CAR I ACTUALLY DROVE:

Slang words or sayings:

"

"

MY CELEBRITY CRUSHES:

A SONG THAT BRINGS BACK MEMORIES:

HISTORIC EVENTS
DURING MY ADULTHOOD

MY FIRST VOTING EXPERIENCE:

A SCARY WORLD EVENT:

How I heard the news:

AN EXCITING AND IMPORTANT EVENT:

How I heard the news:

A NEWSPAPER CLIPPING FROM A MEMORABLE DAY:

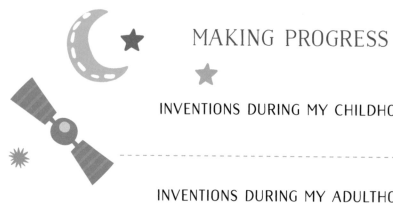

MAKING PROGRESS

INVENTIONS DURING MY CHILDHOOD:

INVENTIONS DURING MY ADULTHOOD:

MY FAVORITE RECENT INVENTION:

HERE'S WHY:

A MODERN GADGET OR GIZMO I COULD DO WITHOUT:

HERE'S WHY:

I HOPE THIS ADVANCEMENT WILL HAPPEN DURING **YOUR** LIFETIME:

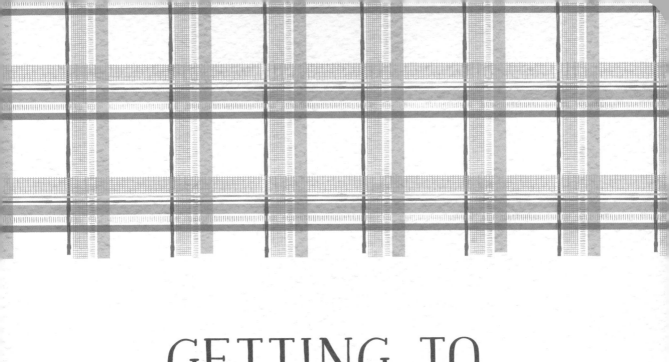

GETTING TO
KNOW ME

WHAT I AM LIKE TODAY

My best personality traits:

MY WORST PERSONALITY TRAITS:

HOW I THINK PEOPLE SEE ME:

HOW I SEE MYSELF:

THE STORY OF *You & Me*

A PERSONALITY TRAIT YOU AND I SHARE:

SOMETHING MANY PEOPLE DON'T REALIZE ABOUT ME:

PLACES I'VE VISITED

SOME FAVORITE AMERICAN DESTINATIONS:

SOME PLACES I HAVE TRAVELED ABROAD:

{ *A memory from a childhood trip:*

--- }

MY ALL-TIME BEST VACATION:

A PLACE I'D LOVE TO VISIT (BUT HAVEN'T YET):

HOBBIES & TALENTS

SOME OF MY HOBBIES & INTERESTS, THROUGH THE YEARS:

A HOBBY OR TWO I WOULD LIKE TO TRY:

A TALENT YOU PROBABLY DON'T KNOW I HAVE:

- -

- -

- -

- -

- -

- -

- -

A PHOTO OF YOUR "TALENTED" GRANDFATHER IN ACTION:

MY SPIRITUAL LIFE

HOW I WOULD CATEGORIZE MY BELIEFS:

....

THE ROLE MY FAITH PLAYED IN MY CHILDHOOD:

....

....

{ *The role spirituality plays in my life today:* }

....

....

MY ADVICE TO YOU ON FAITH:

....

....

....

....

HELPING OTHERS, GIVING BACK

CHARITIES I HAVE SUPPORTED:

- -

- -

VOLUNTEER WORK I HAVE DONE:

- -

- -

I AM GRATEFUL FOR THIS TIME WHEN OTHER PEOPLE HELPED **ME**:

- -

- -

MY ADVICE TO YOU ON ASKING FOR HELP:

- -

- -

- -

- -

MY FAVORITE THINGS NOW

FAVORITE GAMES:

- -

FAVORITE SHOWS OR MOVIES:

- -

Favorite books:

FAVORITE SONGS:

- -

FAVORITE ACTIVITIES AND HOBBIES:

- -

FAVORITE SPORTS AND TEAMS:

- -

Favorite celebrities or heroes:

FAVORITE RELATIVE:

- -

FAVORITE GIFT:

- -

FAVORITE FOODS/BEVERAGES:

- -

FAVORITE THING TO COLLECT:

- -

FAVORITE SLANG OR SAYINGS:

- -

What I disliked as a kid but grew to enjoy as I got older:

TURNING POINTS IN MY LIFE

A BIG DECISION I WAS GLAD I MADE:

- -

WHAT HAPPENED AS A RESULT:

- -

A DECISION I LATER REGRETTED MAKING:

- -

WHAT I LEARNED AS A RESULT:

- -

My advice about choices—and regrets:

- -

- -

- -

BEING YOUR GRANDFATHER

WHEN WE FIRST "MET"

HOW I LEARNED YOU WERE "ON THE WAY":

WHAT I WAS THINKING THE FIRST TIME I HELD YOU:

ME & YOU (AS A BABY):

A PRESENT I GAVE YOU WHEN YOU WERE BORN:

SOME OF THE FIRST TIMES WE SPENT TOGETHER:

WHAT I COULDN'T WAIT TO DO WITH YOU AS YOU GOT OLDER:

OUR SPECIAL BOND

WAYS WE LOOK ALIKE:

WAYS WE ACT ALIKE:

[*My special names for you:*]

WE HAVE THIS SECRET JOKE:

OUR FAVORITE PLACES TO GO AND THINGS TO DO:

....

....

A MEMORY FROM ONE OF OUR BEST DAYS EVER:

....

....

A RECENT PICTURE OF THE TWO OF US:

WHAT YOU HAVE TAUGHT ME

YOU SHOWED ME HOW TO ENJOY THESE THINGS MORE:

- -

- -

- -

You helped me lighten up about these things:

- -

- -

- -

- -

SOMEDAY, I'D LIKE TO TEACH YOU TO:

- -

- -

- -

MY HOPES & DREAMS FOR YOU

MY HOPES FOR YOUR EDUCATION:

FOR YOUR FAMILY:

For your love life:

FOR YOUR CAREER:

THIS IS MY ADVICE ABOUT FOLLOWING YOUR DREAMS:

FROM MY HEART TO YOURS

I MIGHT NOT ALWAYS SAY THESE THINGS,
BUT THEY ARE HERE IN PRINT FOR YOU TO KNOW:

You are _____

You are _____

You are _____

You are _____

You are _____

You are _____

ABOVE ALL, MY GRANDCHILD, *you are loved.*